# Better Vocals Wit

CW00504749

# Rockschool

**A Rockschool Publication**
www.rockschool.co.uk

# Welcome To Level 3 *Female Vocals*

Welcome to the Rockschool Level 3 candidate pack for Female Vocals. This pack includes all the prepared elements needed by a candidate to take grades 6, 7 and 8. In the book you will find exam scores for the performance pieces consisting of a vocal line and chord boxes.

The CDs have backing tracks for the technical exercises and backing tracks for each song. Examples of all the other tests contained in the exam are contained in the accompanying teachers' book.

If you have any queries about this or any other Rockschool exam, please call us on **0845 460 4747** or email us at office@rockschool.co.uk. Visit our website http://www.rockschool.co.uk. Good luck!

## Grade 6

Pieces at this level will be more complex in construction and content and will require a more solid understanding of stylistic matters. The candidate will require knowledge of suitable tone, delivery and rhythm and be expected to portray the song with increasing confidence. The candidate is also expected to demonstrate increasing knowledge of microphone techniques. The candidate will be expected to be able to move effortlessly between registers and to have a wide range of dynamic control and articulation. **All pieces are to be memorised to enable the candidate to gain an increasing sense of performance. A microphone must be used throughout the exam.**

## Grade 7

At this level pieces will be of a substantial length to enable the candidate to demonstrate a thorough working knowledge of suitable stylistic techniques. The pieces will require considerable personal interpretation, with improvisation and ornamentation used to produce a balanced musical result. The candidate is expected to perform the pieces with a considerable sense of commitment and musical integrity and with a well grounded sense of performance and communication. **All pieces are to be memorised to enable the candidate to gain an increasing sense of performance. A microphone must be used throughout the exam.**

## Grade 8

At this level the main emphasis is on performance and this is demonstrated in a complete control of suitable stylistic techniques. The candidate is expected to make full use of microphone techniques to enhance their performance and to demonstrate a secure ability in register and tone. Considerable improvisation and ornamentation is expected to produce an advanced and mature sense of performance with a high degree of personal interpretation. **All pieces are to be memorised to enable the candidate to gain an increasing sense of performance. A microphone must be used throughout the exam.**

### How To Use The CD

The Level 3 book contains two CDs. On these you will find the backing tracks to the exercises and the songs. You should prepare the exercises and the songs using these CDs to perform with in the exam.

For the scales in grades 6, 7 and 8, the first backing track is in the key of A. You will find alternative keys for the scales at the end of the CD in all keys between B♭ and D around middle C. Any of these keys can be used in the exam.

# Important Information For Candidates

Candidates may use this syllabus to enter for either a **grade exam** or a **performance certificate** at grades 6, 7 or 8. If you are entering for a **grade exam**, you will need to prepare the following elements. You will perform them in the exam in the order in which they are shown below. Full syllabus requirements can be found in the *Rockschool Vocal Syllabus Guide* which can be downloaded from www.rockschool.co.uk.

*Technical exercises (10 marks).* You will find two sets of exercises printed for each grade: a scale test and backing tracks exercise.

*General Musicianship Questions (5 marks).* You will be asked five questions at the end of the exam. Three of these will refer to the pieces. You will be asked questions on note values, dynamic markings, articulation markings, key and time signatures and general musical directions. One question will be asked about general vocal technique and a final question on performance and interpretation. Please refer to the *Syllabus Guide* for the GMQ requirements.

*Quick Study Piece (15 marks).* You will be asked to prepare and perform a Quick Study Piece (QSP) in the exam. You should arrive at the exam centre half an hour before your due examination time and you will be given the QSP to practice 20 minutes in advance of entering the exam room. Please refer to the *Syllabus Guide* for the QSP requirements. Examples are printed in the *Companion Guide*.

*Aural Tests (10 marks).* There are two aural tests in each grade. Examples are printed in the *Companion Guide*. The requirements for each grade are as follows:

• **Grade 6**. You will be given a four bar melodic phrase made up of notes and rests. You will also be given a set of rhythmic examples. One of these corresponds to the rests in the melodic phrase. You will select the appropriate test and you will be asked to clap the rest rhythm. The rests will fall on the beat and consist of quaver and crotchet note values. Next you will be given a simple four bar phrase with chord symbols. You will be asked harmonise a simple line after hearing the test three times.

• **Grade 7**. As for Grade 6 but with more complex rhythmic patterns. The rests will fall on and off the beat and consist of quaver and crotchet note values. There will be some note values combined into rests. (2 semiquavers = 1 quaver rest). The 2nd test will be a chord chart. You will hear the complete test once and will be required to sing the bass progression, including 1st inversions, on the repeat. **This test is continuous.**

• **Grade 8**. You will hear an eight bar melody in major or natural minor twice, and will be asked to harmonise a moving line on the 3rd hearing. The 2nd test will be a chord chart in a rhythm. You will hear the complete test once and will be required to sing the bass progression including 1st inversions, on the repeat. **This test is continuous.**

*Three performance pieces (60 marks).* You are not limited solely to the songs printed in this book. You may perform **either** three songs from this book (including one or more from the supplementary list printed for each grade), **or** you may bring in **one** song not included in these lists to perform in the exam. This may be a hit from the chart or a song of your own composing. Please ensure, though, that you have the appropriate backing track. Please turn to the Guru's Guide on page 63 for the list of supplementary material.

If you are entering a **performance certificate**, you will perform five songs, of which up to two may be from repertoire not included in this book or the companion Level 3 volume.

The Level 3 *Female Vocals* book is a companion to the Level 3 *Male Vocals* book. Candidates are welcome to perform repertoire contained in either book in the exam of equivalent difficulty.

# Grade 6 *Technical Exercises*

In this section, the examiner will ask you to perform the two exercises printed below. You do not need to memorise the exercises (and you may use the book in the exam) but the examiner will be looking for the speed and confidence of your response. The examiner will also give you credit for the level of your musicality in your attention to directions, including phrasing and dynamics.

## Exercise 1: Scales

Disc 1 Track 1

You will be asked to perform the following scale and arpeggio exercise beginning on any note between **A-D**. You will be asked to give the exercise *legato* or *staccato* and with *crescendo* and *diminuendo* as directed by the examiner.

## Exercise 2: Backing Vocals

You should prepare all three parts of the following two backing vocal exercises. The examiner will select the part to be given against the other two parts on a backing track. Two examples to be selected.

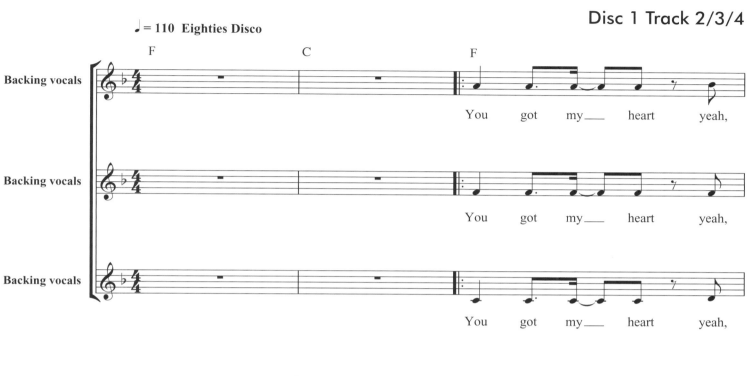

## Exercise 3: Backing Vocals (continued)

Disc 1 Track 5/6/7

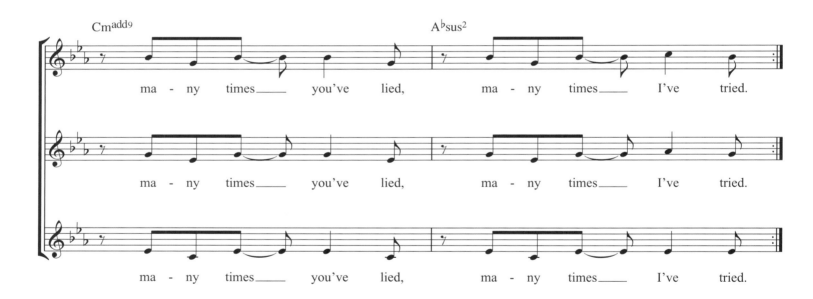

# Rescue Me

Words & Music by
Carl Smith & Raynard Miner

Disc 1 Track 8

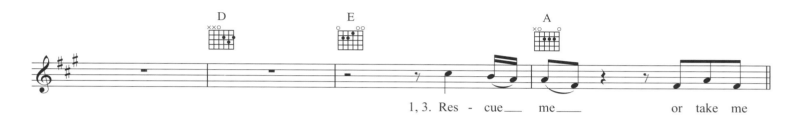

1, 3. Res - cue___ me___ or take me

in your arms,___ res - cue___ me,___ I want your ten - der___ charms___ 'cause I'm a

*(Verse 2 see block lyric)*

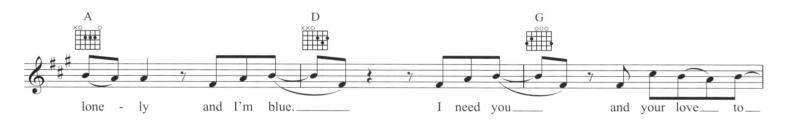

lone - ly and I'm blue.___ I need you___ and your love___ to___

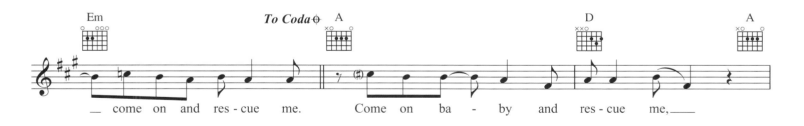

___ come on and res - cue me. Come on ba - by and res - cue me,___

come on ba - by and res - cue me,___ 'cause I need___ you

Verse 2:

Rescue me
Come on and take my heart
Take your love
And comfort every part.

'Cause I'm lonely *etc.*

# Against All Odds (Take A Look At Me Now)

Words & Music by Phil Collins

Disc 1 Track 9

Vocals Level 3 - Female

Verse 3:
I wish I could just make you turn around
Turn around and see me cry.
There's so much I need to say to you
So many reasons why.
You're the only one
Who really knew me at all.

So take a look at me now
Well, there's just an empty space.
There's nothing left here to remind me
Just the memory of you face.
Oh, take a look at me now.
So there's just an empty space.
But to wait for you is all I can do
And that's what I've got to face.

# Man! I Feel Like A Woman!

Words & Music by
Shania Twain & R.J. Lange

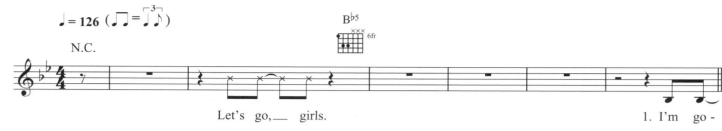

Let's go,___ girls.    1. I'm go-

-ing out to-night, I'm feel-in' al-right; gon-na let it all hang out.___

*(Verses 2 & 3 see block lyric)*

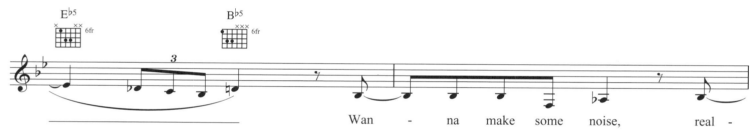

Wan-na make some noise, real-

-ly raise my voice; yeah,___ I wan-na scream and shout.___

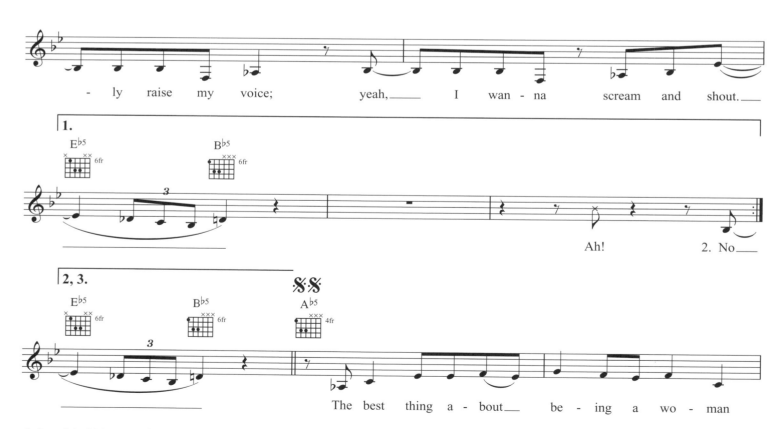

**1.**

Ah!    2. No___

**2, 3.**

The best thing a-bout___ be-ing a wo-man

Vocals Level 3 - Female

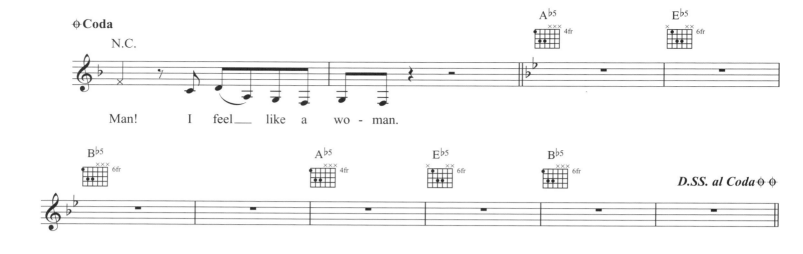

Man! I feel___ like a wo - man.

(Ad lib. vocal)

Man! I feel___ like a wo - man.

I feel like a wo - man.

*Verse 2 :*

No inhibitions
Make no conditions
Get a little outta line.
I ain't gonna act
Politically correct
I only wanna have a good time.

The best thing *etc.*

*Verse 3 :*

The girls need a break.
Tonight we're gonna take
The chance to get out on the town.
We don't need romance
We only wanna dance
We're gonna let our hair hang down.

The best thing *etc.*

Portishead

# All Mine

Words & Music by Geoff Barrow,
Beth Gibbons & Adrian Utley

All the stars ___ may shine ___ a - bright, ___
(*Verse 2 see block lyric*)

___ all the clouds ___ may be white. ___

But when you smile, ___ oh ___ how I ___

___ feel ___ so good ___ that I can hard - ly wait to

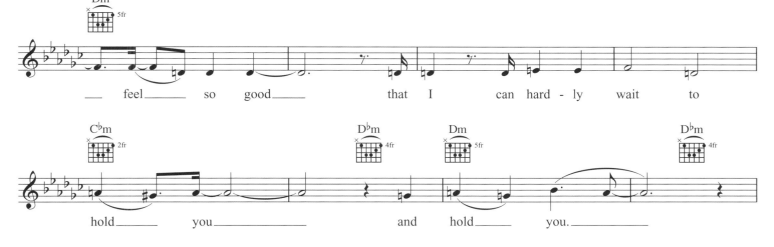

hold ___ you ___ and hold ___ you.

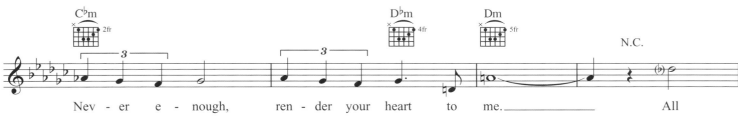

Nev - er e - nough, ren - der your heart to me. ___ All

Vocals Level 3 - Female

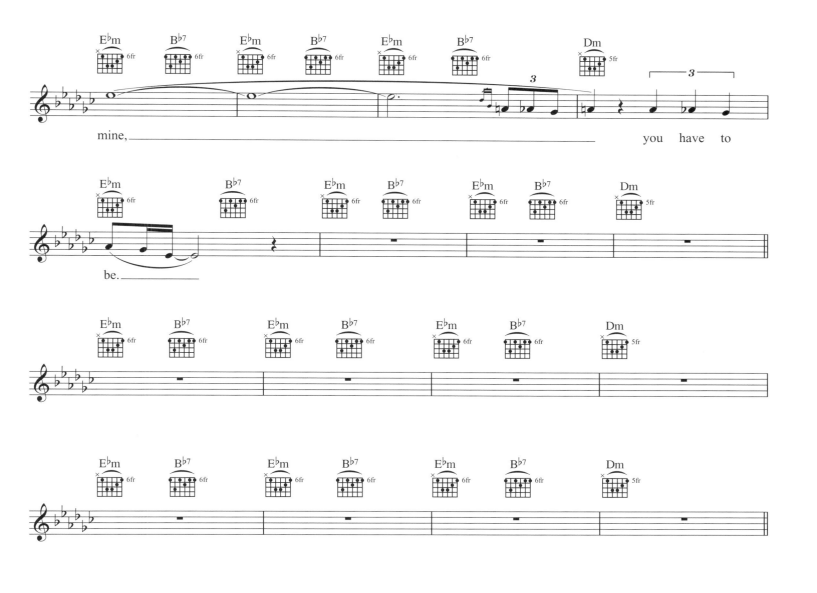

mine,_____ you have to

be._____

*Verse 2:*

From that cloud number nine
Danger starts the sharp incline
And such sad regrets
Oh, as those starry skies
As they swiftly fall.
Make no mistake
You shan't escape
Tethered and tied
There's nowhere to hide from me.

All mine *etc.*

# Survivor

Words & Music by Beyoncé Knowles,
Anthony Dent & Matthew Knowles

1. Now that you're out-ta my life,__ I'm so much bet-ter. You thought that I'd be
*(Verse 2 see block lyric)*

weak with-out____ you, but I'm strong-er. You thought that I'd be

broke____ with-out____ you, but I'm rich-er. You thought that I'd be

sad with-out____ you, I laugh hard-er. Thought I would-n't

grow____ with-out____ you, now I'm wis-er. Thought that I'd be

help-less with-out____ you, but I'm smart-er. You thought that I'd be

stressed with-out____ you, but I'm chill-in'. You thought I would-n't

Vocals Level 3 - Female

Verse 2:

Thought I couldn't breathe without you, I'm inhalin'
Thought I couldn't see without you, perfect vision
Thought I couldn't last without you, but I'm lastin'
Thought that I would die without you, but I'm livin'
Thought that I would fail without you, but I'm on top
Thought that it would be over by now, but it won't stop
Thought that I would self-destruct, but I'm still here
Even in my years to come, I'm still gonna be here.

I'm a survivor *etc.*

# The Winner Takes It All

Words & Music by
Benny Andersson & Bjorn Ulvaeus

1. I don't wanna talk a-bout things

*(Verses 2, 3 & 4 see block lyric)*

we've gone through; though it's hurt-ing me, now it's his-to-ry. I've played all my cards and that's what you've done too, noth-ing more to say noth-ing more to no more ace

Vocals Level 3 - Female

*Verse 2 :*

I was in your arms, thinking I belonged there,
I figured it made sense, building me a fence
Building me a home, thinking I'd be strong there.
But I was a fool, playing by the rules.
The gods may throw a dice, their minds as cold as ice
And someone way down here loses someone dear.
The winner takes it all, the loser has to fall.
It's simple and it's plain, why should I complain?

*Verse 3:*

But tell me, does she kiss like I used to kiss you?
Does it feel the same when she calls your name?
Somewhere deep inside, you must know I miss you.
But what can I say? Rules must be obeyed.
The judges will decide, the likes of me abide
Spectators of the show, always staying low.
The game is on again: a lover or a friend
A big thing or a small, the winner takes it all.

*Verse 4:*

I don't wanna talk if it makes you feel sad.
And I understand you've come to shake my hand.
I apologise if it makes you feel bad
Seeing me so tense, no self-confidence.
The winner takes it all, the winner takes it all.

# Grade 7 *Technical Exercises*

In this section, the examiner will ask you to perform the two exercises printed below. You do not need to memorise the exercises (and you may use the book in the exam) but the examiner will be looking for the speed and confidence of your response. The examiner will also give you credit for the level of your musicality in your attention to directions, including phrasing and dynamics.

## Exercise 1: Scales

Disc 1 Track 14

You will be asked to perform the following scale and arpeggio exercise beginning on any note between **A-D**. You will be asked to give the exercise *legato* or *staccato* and with *crescendo* and *diminuendo* as directed by the examiner.

## Exercise 2: Backing Vocals

You should prepare all three parts of the following two backing vocal exercises. The examiner will select the part to be given against the other two parts on a backing track. Two examples will be selected.

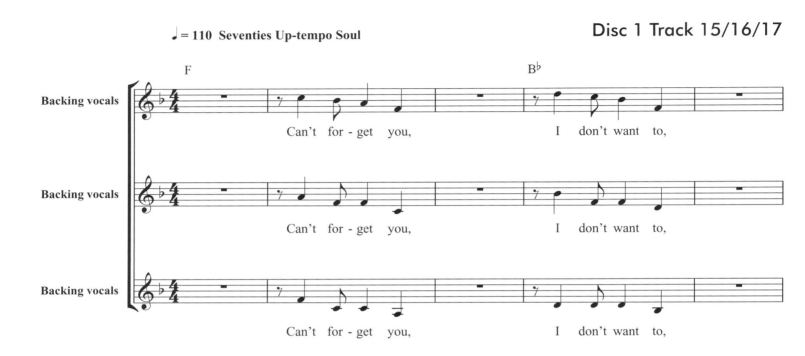

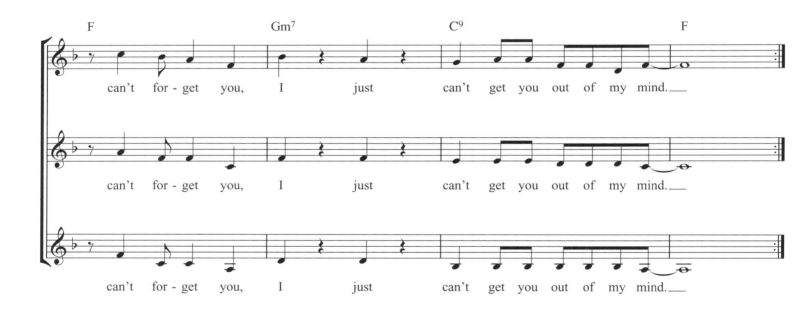

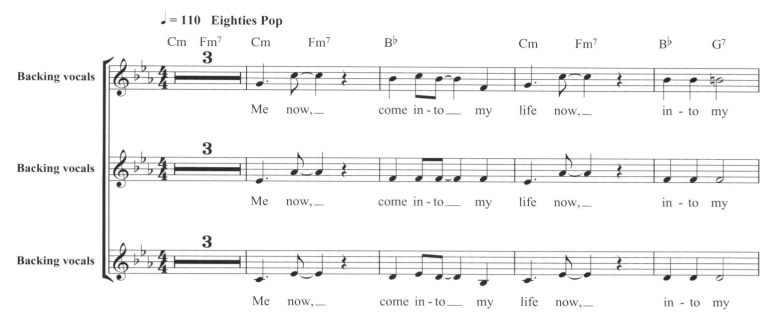

# Saving All My Love For You

Words & Music by
Gerry Goffin & Michael Masser

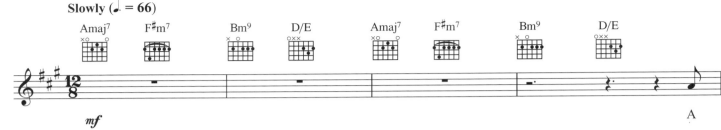

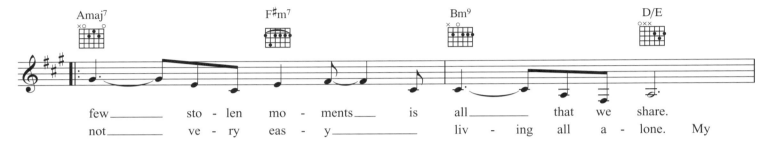

few _____ sto - len mo - ments \_\_\_\_\_ is all \_\_\_\_\_ that we share.
not _____ ve - ry eas - y _____ liv - ing all a - lone. My

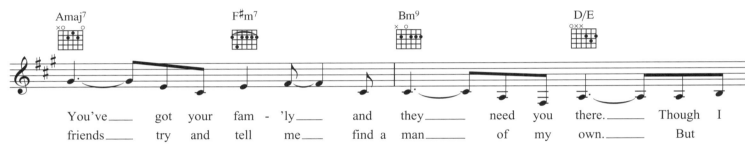

You've \_\_\_\_ got your fam - 'ly \_\_\_\_ and they \_\_\_\_ need you there. \_\_\_\_ Though I
friends \_\_\_\_ try and tell me \_\_\_\_ find a man \_\_\_\_ of my own. \_\_\_\_ But

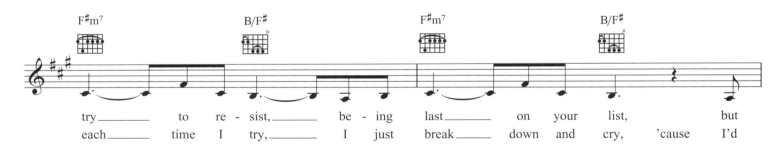

try \_\_\_\_\_ to re - sist, \_\_\_\_\_ be - ing last \_\_\_\_\_ on your list, but
each \_\_\_\_\_ time I try, \_\_\_\_ I just break \_\_\_\_ down and cry, 'cause I'd

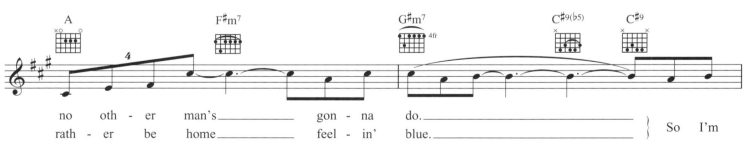

no oth - er man's \_\_\_\_\_ gon - na do.
rath - er be home \_\_\_\_\_ feel - in' blue. \_\_\_\_ So I'm

**1.**

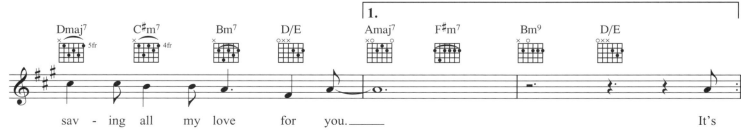

sav - ing all my love for you. \_\_\_\_ It's

Vocals Level 3 - Female

# That Don't Impress Me Much

Words & Music by Shania Twain & R.J. Lange

Disc 1 Track 22

♩ = 124

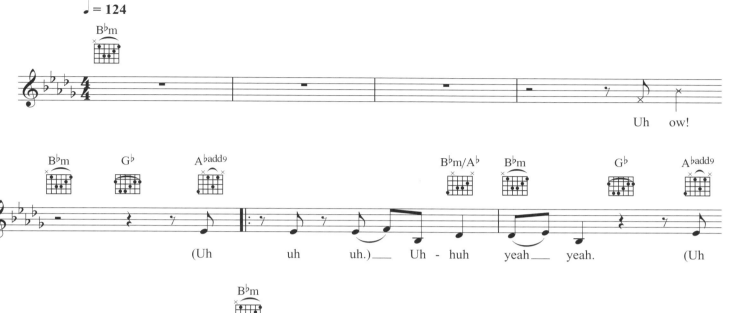

Uh ow!

(Uh   uh   uh.)___ Uh - huh   yeah___ yeah.   (Uh

uh   uh)___ 1. I've   known a   few___ guys who thought they were   pret - ty   smart,___   but

*(Verse 2 see block lyric)*

you've got be - ing   right___ down___ to an art. ___   You   think you're a   ge - nius, you drive me

up   the   wall. ___ You're   a   re - gu - lar o - ri - gi - nal___   know - it - all. ___

Oh, ___   oh,   you   think you're   spe - cial.   Oh, ___   oh,   you   think you're

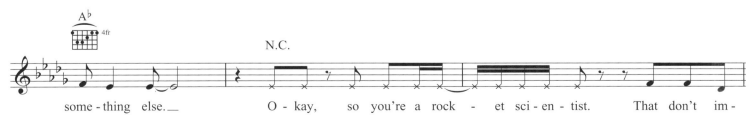

some - thing   else. ___   O - kay,   so you're a rock - et   sci - en - tist.   That don't im -

Vocals Level 3 - Female

# Entering An Exam

Please use one, or a combination, of these forms to enter the exam(s) of your choice. Fill out the details as requested below and send the form, along with the appropriate fees, to:

**Exam Entries, Rockschool Ltd, Evergreen House, 2-4 King Street, Twickenham, Middlesex TW1 3RZ**

There are three examination periods per year for which you may enter. The closing dates for these are shown in the table below.

| PERIOD | DURATION | CLOSING DATE |
|--------|----------|--------------|
| Period A | 1st February to 15th March | 1st December |
| Period B | 15th May to 31st July | 1st April |
| Period C | 1st November to 15th December | 1st October |

You can get up-to-date information on examination prices by ringing the Rockschool help line on **0845 460 4747**
Please make cheques or postal orders payable to **Rockschool Ltd**

# Exam Entry Form

| | |
|---|---|
| **Full Name** | |
| **Address** | |
| | |
| **Post Code** | |
| **Telephone** | |
| **Please tick one** | Grade ☐      Performance Certificates ☐ |
| **Grade** | 1 ☐   2 ☐   3 ☐   4 ☐   5 ☐   6 ☐   7 ☐   8 ☐ |
| **Period** | A ☐      B ☐      C ☐ |
| **Year** | |
| **Fee** | |
| **Dates that are absolutely impossible for you to attend:** | |

# Teacher's Exam Entry Form

Teachers wishing to enter grade exams and performance certificates on behalf of their students should complete the form and send it, along with the appropriate fees, to

**Exam Entries, Rockschool Ltd, Evergreen House, 2-4 King Street, Twickenham, Middlesex TW1 3RZ**

You can get up to date information on examination prices by ringing the Rockschool help line on **0845 460 4747** Please make cheques or postal orders payable to **Rockschool Ltd**

| Teacher's Name |
|---|
| **Address** |
| **Post Code** |
| **Telephone** |

| Name | Grade | Perf.Cert | Period | Year | Fee |
|---|---|---|---|---|---|
|  |  |  |  |  |  |
|  |  |  |  |  |  |
|  |  |  |  |  |  |
|  |  |  |  |  |  |
|  |  |  |  |  |  |
|  |  |  |  |  |  |
|  |  |  |  |  |  |
|  |  |  |  |  |  |
|  |  |  |  |  |  |
|  |  |  |  |  |  |
|  |  |  |  |  |  |
|  |  |  |  |  |  |
|  |  |  |  | **Total fees enclosed** | £ |

**Dates that are absolutely impossible for you to attend:**

**ROCKSCHOOL HELPLINE: 0845 460 4747**
email: **office@rockschool.co.uk**   internet: **www.rockschool.co.uk**

# Vocal Exam Regulations

1. Rockschool exams are open to all persons, irrespective of age.

2. Full payment and relevant documentation must reach the offices of Rockschool on or before the chosen exam period's closing date. Rockschool cannot guarantee an exam for any applications received after this date.

3. Candidates may not transfer an exam from one exam centre to another.

4. Exam entries may not be transferred from one candidate to another.

5. Cancellation of an exam will result in loss of the exam fee unless as a result of illness or injury. Such cases must be substantiated by a medical certificate. In this event, the exam will be re-scheduled on receipt of half of the original exam fee.

6. On application, candidates may state times within an exam period when they are unavailable. However, Rockschool cannot guarantee to avoid all such dates.

7. Rockschool reserves the right to defer exams until the next available exam period. After one deferral, an exam is guaranteed at an exam centre chosen by Rockschool. This may not be your local centre.

8. Candidates must use only the official Rockschool sheet music for their respective exam. Photocopying of any material contained within the official published pack is prohibited. You may not use a Rockschool pack already used by someone else in another exam. This will result in disqualification.

9. No refunds are given.

10. No teacher, or other person, must be present during the preparation of a candidate's Quick Study Piece. Any assistance given to a candidate will result in disqualification from the examination.

11. Only the examiner and candidate are allowed to be present in the examination room with the exception of external moderators or trainee examiners.

12. Candidates must bring in two copies of music for the 'free choice piece'. Players must use an original copy of the tune to be performed, and must provide a second copy for the examiner, which may be a photocopy. If there is no music available, a zero mark will be given for the piece. Any queries in writing should be addressed to the General Manager at least two weeks prior to the exam date.

13. Any special needs candidates must notify the Rockschool office prior to the exam.

14. The examiner's decision is final. Normally, an examiner will hear every component in full, but on occasion an examiner may conclude an examination when a decision has been reached.

15. Rockschool operates a quality assured appeals process, moderated by Trinity College London. All appeals must be made in writing no later than 14 days after the exam date. There are two criteria for formal appeals, these are:
    - Appeals in respect of errors in procedure.
    - Appeals in respect of errors in matching comments to marks awarded.

16. Candidates may use microphones for the lower grades (grades 1-5) but must inform the office of their intention to do so.

# ROCKSCHOOL RESOURCES

At Rockschool we recognise the importance of keeping teachers and learners up to date with developments. Below are listed the qualifications and resources on offer. If you have any questions, please contact us through the relevant email address, or phone us on **0845 460 4747**.

## PERFORMANCE DIPLOMAS

Music Performance Diploma
(DipRSL Perf) at Level 4

Music Performance Licentiate
(LRSL Perf) at Level 6

The Rockschool Performance Diplomas provide flexible, vocationally relevant qualifications for experienced or skilled performers of popular music.

diplomas@rockschool.co.uk

## TEACHING DIPLOMAS

Teaching Diploma
(DipRSL) at Level 4
Teaching Diploma
(LRSL) at Level 6

The Rockschool Teaching Diplomas have been devised for instrumentalists, vocalists and music technologists who would like to attain a teaching qualification without having to attend a course or write essays. The diplomas focus on the practicalities of teaching and are neither genre nor instrument specific.

diplomas@rockschool.co.uk

## MUSIC PRACTITIONERS QUALIFICATIONS

Rockschool/ATM
14-19 Diploma
Compatible

These flexible, vocationally relevant popular music qualifications will provide learners with the necessary skills to develop realistic employment opportunities in the music industry.

qualifications@rockschool.co.uk

## COMPANION GUIDES

Sight Reading (Grades 1-8)
Improvisation & Interpretation
(Grades 1-5)
QSPs (Grades 6-8)
Ear Tests (Grades 1-8)
GMQs (Grades 1-8)

A must for any music teacher or self-taught musician using the Rockschool grade system. Rockschool Companion Guides contain examples of the exercises you will encounter in an exam along with tips on how best to perform.

info@rockschool.co.uk

Companion Guides available for purchase through **www.musicroom.com**

## GUITAR DVDS

Following DVDs available:
Grades Debut & 1
Grade 2
Grade 3

Perfect for anyone working through the Rockschool grades, Rockschool DVDs include instructional lessons on how to make the most of the pieces and technical exercises required in your exams.

info@rockschool.co.uk

DVDs available for purchase through **www.musicroom.com**

## COMING SOON...REPERTOIRE BOOKS

Rockschool Repertoire Books contain popular songs from rock through to indie. **Drums Grades 1 to 3** will be available from October 2008.

info@rockschool.co.uk

Repertoire Books soon available for purchase through **www.musicroom.com**

Verse 2:

I never knew a guy who carried a mirror in his pocket
And a comb up his sleeve, just in case.
And all that extra-hold gel in your hair oughta lock it
'Cause heaven forbid it should fall outa place!

Oh, oh, you think you're special.
Oh, oh, you think you're something else.
Okay, so you're Brad Pitt.

That don't impress me much *etc.*

# Midnight Train To Georgia

Words & Music by Jim Weatherly

34 © Copyright 1971 Bibo Music Publishing Incorporated, USA.
Universal Music Publishing Limited.
All Rights Reserved. International Copyright Secured.

This music is copyright. Photocopying is illegal.

Verse 2:

He kept dreamin' that someday he'd be the star
(A superstar, but he didn't get far)
But he sure found out the hard way
That dreams don't always come true
So he turned all his hopes
And he even sold his old car
Bought a one-way ticket back to the life he once knew.

He's leavin' *etc.*

# Respect

Words & Music by Otis Redding

**Solid 4 Beat**

What you want ba-by I got.
I ain't gon-na do you wrong while you gone.

What you need you know I got it.
I ain't gon-na do you wrong 'cause I don't wan-na.

All I'm ask-in' is for a lit-tle re-spect, when you come home. Ba-

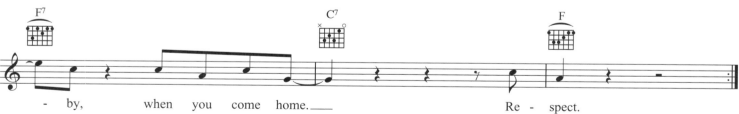

- by, when you come home.___ Re-spect.

I'm out___ to give you all my mon-ey,
Ooh,___ your kiss-es, sweet-er than hon-ey,

36

but all I'm ask - in'     in re - turn, hon - ey,
but guess____ what,____     so here's my mon - ey,

is to give me     my prop - er re - spect when you get
all I want you to do for me     is give me some here when you get

home.     Yeah, ba - by, when you get home.
home.     Yeah, ba - by, when you get home.

**1.** F#m     B     F#m     G⁷

**2.**

C⁷     F

R - E - S - P - E - C - T,     find out what it means to me,

C⁷     F

R - E - S - P - E - C - T,     take out T - C - P,

C⁷     F

*Repeat and fade out*

a lit - tle re - spect.

# All I Really Want

Words by Alanis Morissette
Music by Alanis Morissette & Glen Ballard

1. Do I

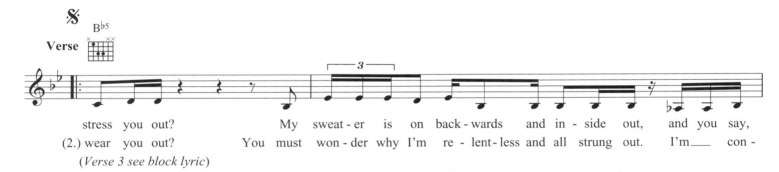

stress you out? My sweat-er is on back-wards and in-side out, and you say,
(2.) wear you out? You must won-der why I'm re-lent-less and all strung out. I'm con-
*(Verse 3 see block lyric)*

"how _____ ap - pro - pri - ate." I
- sumed by the chill of sol - i - tar - y. _____ I'm like E -

don't want to di - sect ev - 'ry-thing to - day. I don't mean to pick you a - part, you see, but I
- stel - la. I like to reel it in, and then spit it out. I'm frus -

can't _____ help _____ it. 1. And
- trat - ed by your a - pa - thy. 2. And

Vocals Level 3 - Female

**Bridge**

-nough a - bout me, let's talk a - bout you___ for a min - ute. E -

-nough a - bout you, let's talk a - bout life___ for a while;___ the con -

-flicts, the craz - i - ness, the sound___ of pre - tens - es fall - ing all___ a - round,___

*D.S. al Coda*

___ all___ a - round.___

**Coda**

**Chorus**

real - ly want is some___ peace man,___ a

real - ly want is some___ com - fort,___ a

all I really want is some patience, a way to calm me down. And

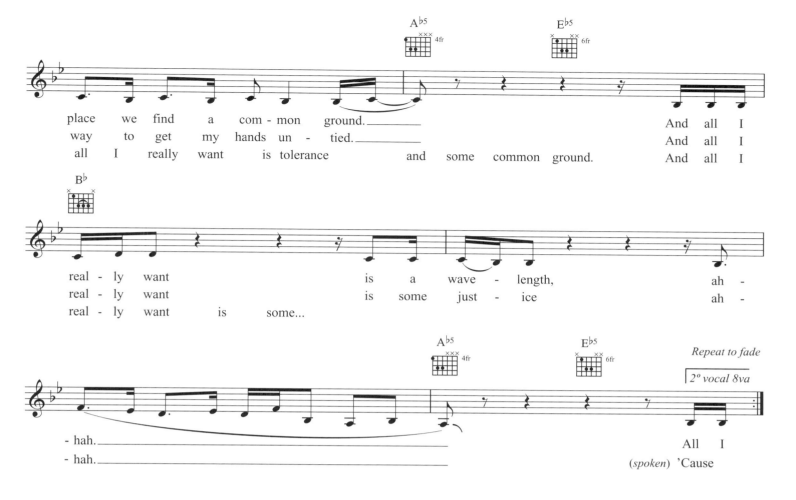

place we find a com-mon ground._____ And all I
way to get my hands un - tied._____ And all I
all I really want is tolerance and some common ground. And all I

real - ly want is a wave - length, ah -
real - ly want is some just - ice ah -
real - ly want is some...

- hah._____ All I
- hah._____ (spoken) 'Cause

*Repeat to fade*
*2° vocal 8va*

*Verse 3 (𝄋):*

Why are you so petrified of slience?
Here, can you handle this?
Did you think about your bills, your ex, your deadlines
Or when you think you're gonna die?
Or did you long for the next distraction?

*Pre-chorus 3:*

And all I need now is intellectual intercourse
A soul to dig the hole much deeper.
And I have no concept of time other that it is flying
If only I could kill the killer.

# Emotion

Words & Music by
Barry Gibb & Robin Gibb

Yeah yeah___ yeah yeah___ yeah___ ooh yeah.___

___ 1. It's o - ver and done___ but the heart - ache lives on___ in - side.___

(*Verse 2 see block lyric*)

___ And who is the one you're cling - ing___ to___ in - stead of me to -

- night?___ And where are you now,___ now that I need___

___ you?___ Tears on my pil - low___ wher - ev - er you go,___ go___ I'll cry me a ri -

- ver___ that leads to your o - cean.___ You ne - ver see me fall a - part,___ in the

words of a bro - ken heart it's just e - mo - tions ta - ken me o - ver, caught up in sor -

Vocals Level 3 - Female

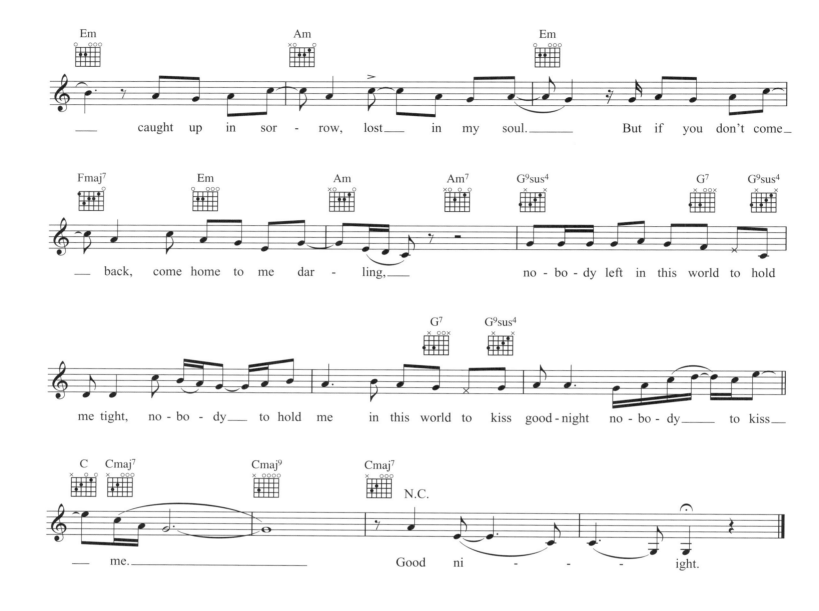

*Verse 2*:

I'm there at your side,
I'm part of all the things you are
But you've got a part of someone else
You've got to go find your shining star

And where are you now  *etc.*

# Grade 8 *Technical Exercises*

In this section, the examiner will ask you to perform the two exercises printed below. You do not need to memorise the exercises (and you may use the book in the exam) but the examiner will be looking for the speed and confidence of your response. The examiner will also give you credit for the level of your musicality in your attention to directions, including phrasing and dynamics.

## Exercise 1: Scales

Disc 2 Track 1

You will be asked to perform the following scale and arpeggio exercise beginning on any note between **A-D**. You will be asked to give the exercise *legato* or *staccato* and with *crescendo* and *diminuendo* as directed by the examiner

Continues overleaf

## Exercise 2: Backing Vocals

You should prepare all three parts of the following two backing vocal exercises. The examiner will select the part to be given against the other two parts on a backing track. Two examples will be selected.

♩ = 100   Seventies Funk

Disc 2 Track 2/3/4

## Exercise 2: Backing Vocals (continued)

# How Come You Don't Call Me

Words & Music by Prince

*Spoken:* But all wanna know baby is if what we had is good… Oh, ___ oh, oh, oh.

Mm. Ah.

Yeah, ___ ba - by. "Uh, let me tell you something."

1. I keep your ___ pic - ture be - side ___ my ___ bed. ___ Mm.
*(Verse 2 see block lyric)*

And I still re - mem - ber ev - 'ry - thing ___ you said. ___

___ Mm. ___ Oh. ___ I al - ways thought our ___ love ___

___ was so ___ right, I guess I was wrong. ___ Mm, ___ mm.

Vocals Level 3 - Female

oh._____ Ooh,_____ won't you call me some - time, pa - pa?_____

*Vocal ad lib.*

Why_____ on earth can't you just pick up the phone?_ You know I don't

*Repeat ad lib. to fade*

like to be a - lone._____ How come you don't call me "why must you torture me?"

*Verse 2*:

Still light the fire on the rainy night
Still like it better when you're holding me tight
Everybody said
Everybody said that we should never part
Tell me baby, baby, baby why
Why you wanna go and break my heart.

All I wanna know baby *etc.*

# Hero

Words & Music by
Mariah Carey & Walter Afanasieff

Moderately

mp

1. There's a

he - ro if you look in - side____ your heart. You don't
2. long____ road when you face the world____ a - lone. No one

have to be____ a - fraid of what you are.____ There's an an -
reach - es out a hand for you to hold._____ You can find____

- swer if you reach in - to____ your soul_____ and the
____ love if you search with - in____ your - self_____ and the

sor - row that____ you know____ will melt a - way.
emp - ti - ness____ you felt____ will dis - ap - pear.

And then a he - ro comes____ a - long____ with the strength to car - ry on____

____ and you cast your fears____ a - side____ and you know you can sur - vive.____

Vocals Level 3 - Female

# Shoulda Woulda Coulda

Words & Music by
Beverley Knight & Craig Wiseman

1. Peo - ple say that to - geth - er we were both sides___ of the same coin,___
*(Verses 2 & 3 see block lyrics)*

that we would shine like__ Ve - nus in a clear night sky.___ We thought our love__

__ could ov - er - come the cir - cum - stan - ces,___ but my__ am - bi -

- tion would - n't al - low___ for com - pro - mise.___

And how I wish I,___ wish I'd done a lit - tle bit

more.___ Now should - a, would - a, could - a means I'm out of time.

Vocals Level 3 - Female

Should - a, would - a, could - a are the last words of\_ a fool.\_

I wish I,_____ wish I'd done a lit - tle bit

more._____ Now\_ should - a, would - a, could - a means I'm out of time.

Should - a, would - a, could - a can't change your mind.\_ And I won - der,\_ won - der what I'm gon - na do.\_

Should - a, would - a, could - a can't change your mind.\_ Should - a, would - a, could - a means I'm out of time.

Should - a, would - a, could - a can't change your_____ mind._____

Oh,\_ can't change your\_\_\_\_ mind._____

*Verse 2:*
I could see in the distance all the dreams that were clear to me
Every choice that I had to make left you on your own
Somehow the road we started down had split asunder
Too late to realise how far apart we'd grown.

And how I wish *etc.*

*Verse 3:*
People ask how it feels to live the kind of life others dream about
I tell them everybody gotta face their highs and their lows
And in my life there's a love that I put aside, 'cause I was busy loving something else
So for every little thing you hold on to, you've got to let something else go.

And how I wish *etc.*

# The Reason

Words & Music by Carole King,
Mark Hudson & Greg Wells

Disc 2 Track 11

Vocals Level 3 - Female

Verse 2:

I'm giving it up
No more running around spinning my wheel
You came out of my dream and made it real
I know what I feel, it's you,
It's all bcause of you.

# I Will Always Love You

Words & Music by Dolly Parton

Vocals Level 3 - Female

# The Guru's Guide To Level 3 *Female Vocals*

## Supplementary Material

Rockschool recommends the following songs in addition to the repertoire printed in this book.  The list below shows the songs arranged by grade along with the publications in which they may be found.

### Grade 6

| | | |
|---|---|---|
| Chain Of Fools | *All Woman Soul* | IMP9668A |
| Flashdance… What A Feeling | *All Woman 2* | IMP7268A |
| My Baby Just Cares for Me | *Essential Audition Songs: Jazz Standards* | IMP7021A |
| My Heart Will Go On | *Essential Audition Songs: Pop Ballads* | IMP6939A |
| Get Here | *All Woman 1* | IMP7077A |
| Evergreen | *All Woman 4* | IMP9255A |
| What's Love Got To Do With It? | *All Woman 1* | IMP7077A |
| Touch Me In The Morning | *All Woman 4* | IMP9255A |
| Don't Know Why | *All Woman Songbirds* | IMP9914A |
| Out Here On My Own | *Professional Singer's Audition Book* | AM966680 |
| Walk On By | *Essential Audition Songs: Pop Ballads* | IMP6939A |
| If I Could Turn Back Time | *All Woman 4* | IMP9255A |
| Rainy Night In Georgia | *All Woman 4* | IMP9255A |

### Grade 7

| | | |
|---|---|---|
| Feeling Good | *You're The Voice: Nina Simone* | IMP9606A |
| Misled | *You're The Voice: Celine Dion* | IMP9297A |
| Lady Marmalade | *All Woman Soul* | IMP9668A |
| Do You Know Where You're Going To | *Essential Audition Songs: Pop Ballads* | IMP6939A |
| Who's Zoomin' Who? | *You're The Voice: Aretha Franklin* | IMP9349A |
| Show Me Heaven | *Professional Singer's Audition Book* | AM966680 |

### Grade 8

| | | |
|---|---|---|
| The Power Of Love | *You're The Voice: Celine Dion* | IMP9297A |
| Unbreak My Heart | *Essential Audition Songs: Pop Divas* | IMP7769A |
| I Turn To You | *Audition Songs For Female Singers  11* | AM959156 |
| Total Eclipse Of The Heart | *All Woman 3* | IMP9187A |
| Think | *You're The Voice: Aretha Franklin* | IMP9349A |

## Warm Up

It is important that you prepare for the exam by warming up your voice properly.  You should ensure that you arrive at the exam centre within plenty of time to do this.  We have arranged the elements of the grade exam such that the performances come at the end.  The backing tracks and/or accompaniment are always variable in volume and you should always tell the examiner if you feel that you are straining to be heard.

## Free Choice Pieces

In grade exams you are allowed to perform one song not specified in this book.  This may be a hit from the chart or a song composed by yourself.  In performance certificate exams you are allowed to perform up to two songs not specified in this book.

If you wish to find out whether a free choice piece song is appropriate for the grade, you may either contact Rockschool and submit the song for adjudication, or look on our website www.rockschool.co.uk and consult the free choice piece criteria.

## Marking Schemes

The table below shows the marking schemes for grad exams and performance certificates. All Rockschool exams are marked out of 100 and the pass mark for a grade exam is 65% and for a performance certificate is 70%.

### *Grade Exam*

| Element | Pass | Merit | Distinction |
|---|---|---|---|
| Technical Exercises | 6 out of 10 | 7 out of 10 | 8 out of 10 |
| General Musicianship Questions | 3 out of 5 | 4 out of 5 | 5 out of 5 |
| Aural Tests | 6 out of 10 | 7 out of 10 | 8 out of 10 |
| Quick Study Piece | 11 out of 15 | 12 out of 15 | 13 out of 15 |
| Piece 1 | 13 out of 20 | 15 out of 20 | 17 out of 20 |
| Piece 2 | 13 out of 20 | 15 out of 20 | 17 out of 20 |
| Piece 3 | 13 out of 20 | 15 out of 20 | 17 out of 20 |

### *Performance Certificate*

| Element | Pass | Merit | Distinction |
|---|---|---|---|
| Piece 1 | 14 out of 20 | 16 out of 20 | 18 out of 20 |
| Piece 2 | 14 out of 20 | 16 out of 20 | 18 out of 20 |
| Piece 3 | 14 out of 20 | 16 out of 20 | 18 out of 20 |
| Piece 4 | 14 out of 20 | 16 out of 20 | 18 out of 20 |
| Piece 5 | 14 out of 20 | 16 out of 20 | 18 out of 20 |

## Examination Criteria

Rockschool examiners assess all examinations according to strict guidelines. Copies of these for vocals can be found on the website www.rockschool.co.uk or direct from our offices. Please ring **0845 460 4747** for further details.

## Exam Regulations

Entering a Rockschool exam is easy. Please read through the instructions on the back of the entry form accompanying this book carefully, before filling it in. Information on current fees can be obtained by ringing Rockschool on **0845 460 4747** or by logging on to the website www.rockschool.co.uk.